W9-DEF-691

A Basket of Friends

A Little Book of Friendship & Inspiration

To My Daughter-in-law

Stephanie

with Love

ISBN 1-57051-066-0

Cover/Interior: Koechel Peterson & Associates

Printed in the USA

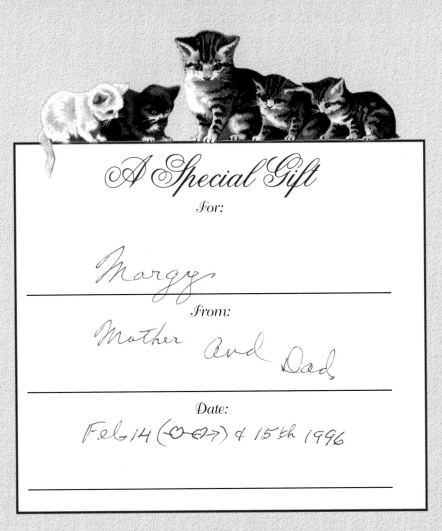

A Special Gift

For:

Marggg

From:

Mother and Dad

Date:

Feb 14 (♡←⊙→) & 15th 1996

Cherished Moments
Gift Books

A Basket of Friends

Merry Christmas With Love

Once Upon a Memory

Sweet Rose of Friendship

Tea for Two

Where Angels Dwell

A Basket of Friends

Edited by Paul C. Brownlow

Brownlow

BROWNLOW PUBLISHING COMPANY, INC.

Cats and Kittens: Objects of Our Affections

The ancient kingdom of Egypt was the first known civilization to enjoy and cultivate the cat. The Egyptians even worshiped gods that were made in the image of a cat's head. Later, Greek merchants transported the cat throughout Asia Minor, the coast of North Africa, and the western Mediterranean. The Romans, in their turn, took the cat with them as they expanded and conquered the world.

During the Middle Ages, cats (and black cats in particular) were considered evil and thus persecuted. Cats, thought to be witches in disguise or agents of Satan, were killed and ritually put to death. The cat became almost extinct in Europe.

European Crusaders returning from the Holy Land brought rats and the Bubonic Plague with them. In response to the devastating plague, cats were restored to their former honor by helping to exterminate the rodents and stop the crisis.

During the eighteenth century, cats became the subject of English poetry and paintings. The first cat show was organized in London in 1851 by Harrison Weir. Edinburgh hosted a Scottish cat show in 1875, and the Americans did likewise in 1895. The cat was once again a protected pet and object of human affections.

Few animals exhibit more maternal tenderness, or show a greater love for their offspring, than the mother cat. The assiduity with which she attends them and the pleasure which she seems to take in all their playful tricks afford a grateful entertainment to every observer.

REVEREND W. BINGLEY, 1824

Once it [a cat] has given its love, what absolute confidence, what fidelity of affection! It will make itself the companion of your hours of work, of loneliness, or of sadness. It will lie the whole evening on your knee, purring and happy in your society, and leaving the company of creatures of its own society to be with you.

THEOPHILE GAUTIER

An Affectionate Unity

Friendship is the affectionate unity, which exists between two or more and endears them to each other, by the strongest ties. There may be felt in true friendship some of the most pure and disinterested emotions that this earth can afford. But we should be careful, and select only wise and virtuous for our companions; and put confidence in none but those whom we have learned to be true by a long acquaintance. There are many who are friends (or pretend to be) in prosperity but if adversity should visit us, will forsake us, and we cannot consider them as real friends. It is those who will stand by us in trouble as well as in prosperity, who will sympathize with us in affliction and pour consolation into our bosoms, that we should prize above all others. That such may be yours is the wish of your sincere friend…

HARRIET B. DAVIS MINOT

The Cat Who Came to Tea

When the tea is brought at five o'clock,
And all the neat curtains are drawn with care,
The little black cat with bright green eyes
Is suddenly purring there.

HAROLD MONRO

I always felt that the great high privilege,
relief and comfort of friendship
was that one had to explain nothing.

KATHERINE MANSFIELD

Let Me Be Aware

God—let me be aware.

Let me not stumble blindly down the ways,

Just getting somehow safely through the days,

Not even groping for another hand,

Not even wondering why it all was planned,

Eyes to the ground unseeking for the light,

Soul never aching for a wild-winged flight;

Please, keep me eager just to do my share.

God—let me be aware.

MIRIAM TEICHNER

The only thing that makes one place more attractive to me than another is the quantity of heart I find in it.

JANE WELSH CARLYLE

Cats seem to go on the principle that it never does any harm to ask for what you want.

JOSEPH WOOD KRUTCH

Good communication is as stimulating as black coffee, and just as hard to sleep after.

ANNE MORROW LINDBERGH

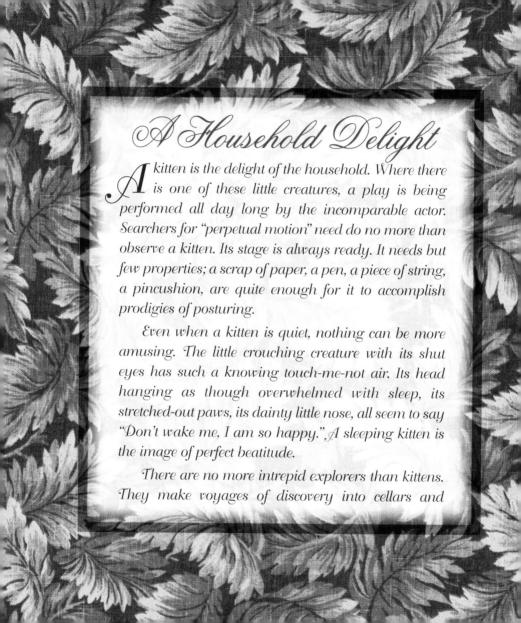

A Household Delight

A kitten is the delight of the household. Where there is one of these little creatures, a play is being performed all day long by the incomparable actor. Searchers for "perpetual motion" need do no more than observe a kitten. Its stage is always ready. It needs but few properties; a scrap of paper, a pen, a piece of string, a pincushion, are quite enough for it to accomplish prodigies of posturing.

Even when a kitten is quiet, nothing can be more amusing. The little crouching creature with its shut eyes has such a knowing touch-me-not air. Its head hanging as though overwhelmed with sleep, its stretched-out paws, its dainty little nose, all seem to say "Don't wake me, I am so happy." A sleeping kitten is the image of perfect beatitude.

There are no more intrepid explorers than kittens. They make voyages of discovery into cellars and *garrets, they climb on the roofs of neighbouring houses, put their little noses out of half-closed street doors, and return with a store of observation laid up for future use. Sometimes, however, this ardent curiosity leads them into dangerous places, and brings them into difficulties which they have cause to regret.*

CHAMPFLEURY (JULES HUSSON)

For the Love of a Friend

Oh, for the love of a friend whose voice and touch will rainbow sorrows, diamond tears, making of them gems of rarest joy; one who forgives all my shortages ere asked to do so; one who dares to the uttermost of human imagery; one whose ship will cast anchor, and throw out the life line of hope when storms are near; one who forgives in me all that I can forgive in myself. Oh, for the love of a friend who can be made the sacred trustee of my heart; one who is more to me than the closest relative; one whose very name is so sacred that I want to whisper it softly; one who lingers near my door in time of distress, and stretches forth his hand, which is not empty or cold, and who says little, but feels largely.

MAE LAWSON

*The cure for anything is
salt water—sweat, tears, or the sea.*

ISAK DINESEN

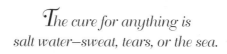

*I sprang to life with playful merry face,
The prettiest kitten of my pretty race;
My mother purr'd her joys with fond surprise
And watched with anxious care my opening eyes.*

CHARLES LAMB

*We can all be servants of God
wherever our lot is cast;
but He gives us different sorts of work
according as He fits us for it,
and calls us to it.*

GEORGE ELIOT

Lord,
Love Through Me

Love this world through me, Lord.

This world of broken men,

Thou didst love through death, Lord.

Oh, love in me again!

Souls are in despair, Lord.

Oh, make me know and care;

When my life they see,

May they behold Thee.

Oh, love the world through me.

WILL HOUGHTON

A Day Well Spent

If you sit down at set of sun
And count the acts that you have done,
And, counting, find one self-denying deed, one word
That eased the heart of him who heard—
One glance most kind,
That fell like sunshine where it went—
Then you may count that day well spent.

GEORGE ELIOT

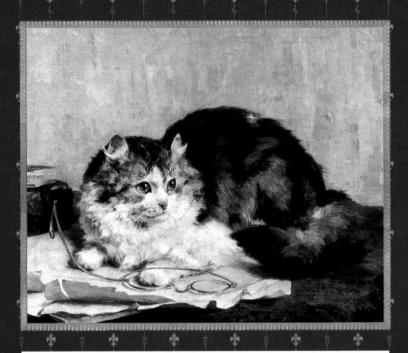

*Most people are just like cats in that if you rub them
the right way, they will purr. But if you rub them
the wrong way, they will bite and scratch.*

WILLIAM ROSS

Friendship of a kind that cannot
easily be reversed tomorrow must have its roots
in common interests and shared beliefs.

BARBARA TUCHMAN

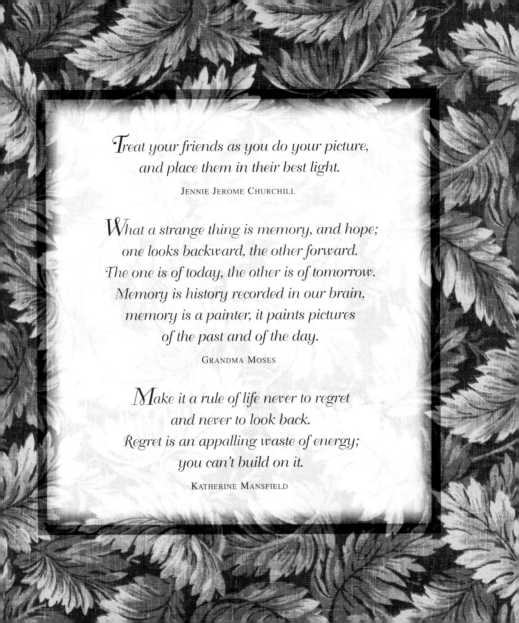

*Treat your friends as you do your picture,
and place them in their best light.*

JENNIE JEROME CHURCHILL

*What a strange thing is memory, and hope;
one looks backward, the other forward.
The one is of today, the other is of tomorrow.
Memory is history recorded in our brain,
memory is a painter, it paints pictures
of the past and of the day.*

GRANDMA MOSES

*Make it a rule of life never to regret
and never to look back.
Regret is an appalling waste of energy;
you can't build on it.*

KATHERINE MANSFIELD

We are all fellow passengers on the same planet, and we are all equally responsible for the happiness and the well-being of the world in which we happen to live.

HENDRICK VAN LOON

*I am convinced
that we must train
not only the head,
but the heart
and hand as well.*

MADAME CHIANG KAI-SHEK

❧

*God made the cat in order
that man might have the pleasure
of caressing the lion.*

FERNAND MERY

❧

*To be capable of
steady friendship or lasting love
are the two greatest proofs,
not only of goodness of heart,
but of strength of mind.*

WILLIAM HAZLITT

*M*ake the attempt if you want to, but you will find
that trying to go through life without friendship
is like milking a bear to get cream for your
morning coffee. It is a whole lot of trouble,
and then not worth much after you get it.

ZORA NEALE HURSTON

At my table, sit with me.
I'll pour coffee or some tea.
Perhaps we'll share our tears and laughter,
And be friends forever after.

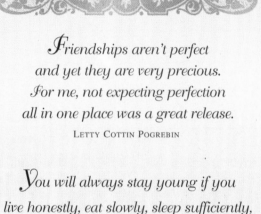

*Friendships aren't perfect
and yet they are very precious.
For me, not expecting perfection
all in one place was a great release.*

LETTY COTTIN POGREBIN

*You will always stay young if you
live honestly, eat slowly, sleep sufficiently,
work industriously, worship faithfully—
and lie about your age.*

*Let love and faithfulness never leave you;
bind them around your neck,
write them on the tablet of your heart.*

PROVERBS 3:3

There can be no happiness equal to the joy of finding a heart that understands.

VICTOR ROBINSALL

The Kitten

See the kitten on the wall,
Sporting with the leaves that fall,
Withered leaves, one, two, and three
Falling from the elder tree,
Through the calm and frosty air
Of the morning bright and fair.

See the kitten, how she starts,
Crouches, stretches, paws and darts;
With a tiger-leap half way
Now she meets her coming prey.
Lets it go as fast and then
Has it in her power again.

Now she works with three and four,
Like an Indian conjurer;
Quick as he in feats of art,
Gracefully she plays her part;
Yet were gazing thousands there;
What would little Tabby care?

WILLIAM WORDSWORTH

When Souls Mingle

What we ordinarily call friends and friendships are nothing but acquaintanceships and
familiarities formed by some chance or convenience, by
means of which our souls are bound to each other. In
the friendship I speak of, our souls mingle and blend
with each other so completely that they efface the seam
that joined them, and cannot find it again. If you press
me to tell why I loved him, I feel that this cannot be
expressed, except by answering: Because it was he,
because it was I.

MICHEL DE MONTAIGNE

Three Little Kittens

Three little kittens lost their mittens,
And they began to cry:
"O, mother dear,
We sadly fear,
That we have lost our mittens!"

"Lost your mittens, you naughty kittens!
Then you shall have no pie!"
"Meeow, meeow, meeow!"
"No, you shall have no pie."
"Meeow, meeow, meeow!"

The three little kittens found their mittens,
And they began to cry,
"O mother dear,
See here, see here!
See, we have found our mittens!"

Cats

leave

paw prints

on our

hearts.

*Little George was
visiting his aunt.
He found the cat in a sunny
window purring cheerfully.
"Oh, Auntie, come quick,"
said Little George,
"the cat has gone to sleep
and left his engine running."*

*Never undertake anything
for which you wouldn't have
the courage to ask
the blessings of Heaven.*

*The human heart
yearns for the beautiful
in all ranks of life.*

HARRIET BEECHER STOWE

*Believe only half of what you see
and nothing that you hear.*

DINAH MULOCK CRAIK

*Intimacies between women
often go backwards,
beginning in revelations
and ending in small talk.*

ELIZABETH BOWEN

*Those who dwell among the
beauties and mysteries of the earth
are never alone or weary of life.*

RACHEL CARSON

Nothing Sweeter

Nothing is sweeter than love, nothing stronger,
nothing higher, nothing wider, nothing more pleasant,
nothing fuller or better in heaven or on earth.
Love often knows no limits but is fervent
beyond measure. Love feels no burden,
thinks nothing of labors, attempts what is above
its strength, pleads no excuse of impossibility....
Though wearied, it is not tired; though pressed,
it is not straitened; though alarmed, it is not confounded;
but as a lively flame and burning torch, it forces
its way upwards and passes securely through all.

THOMAS À KEMPIS

Thank You, Friend

I never came to you, my friend,
And went away without
Some new enrichment of the heart:
More faith, and less of doubt,
More courage for the days ahead,
And often in great need
Coming to you, I went away
Comforted, indeed.

How can I find the shining words,
The glowing phrase that tells
All that your love has meant to me,
All that your friendship spells?
There is no word, no phrase for you
On whom I so depend.
All I can say to you is this:
God bless you, precious friend.

GRACE NOLL CROWELL

*I*f you approach each new person in a spirit of adventure, you will find yourself endlessly fascinated by the new channels of thought and experience and personality that you encounter.

ELEANOR ROOSEVELT

Confront a child, a puppy, and a kitten with a sudden danger; the child will turn instinctively for assistance, the puppy will grovel in abject submission…the kitten will brace its tiny body for a frantic resistance.

SAKI

Look Into My Heart

*N*ow in all matters, hypocrisy is vicious (for it distorts and destroys our judgment), but is particularly hostile to friendship, for it makes honesty impossible, and without honesty the word "friendship" has no meaning. For the essence of friendship consists in the fact that many souls, so to speak, become one, and how can that take place if even in the one individual the soul is not single and forever the same, but various, changeable, kaleidoscopic?

For in friendship unless you see the naked heart and let your own be seen, there is nothing that you can deem trustworthy or reliable, not even the mere fact of loving and being loved, since you cannot know how genuine the sentiment is.

CICERO

The Maternal Cat

An old lady cat felt that she was dying, before her kittens were weaned. She could hardly walk, but she disappeared one morning, carrying a kitten, and came back without it. Next day, quite exhausted, she did this with her other two kittens, and then died. She had carried each kitten to a separate cat, each of which was nourishing a family, and accepted the new fosterling. Can anything be wiser or more touching?

ANDREW LANG

Soul of My Soul

Soul of my soul, my Joy, my Crown, my Friend,

A name which all the rest doth comprehend;

How happy are we now, whose souls are grown,

By an incomparable mixture, one:

Whose well-acquainted minds are now as near

As Love, or Vows, or Friendship can endear?

I have no thought but what's to thee reveal'd,

Nor thou desire that is from me conceal'd.

Thy heart locks up my secrets richly set,

And my breast is thy private cabinet.

KATHERINE PHILIPS

*To understand any living
thing you must creep within and
feel the beating of its heart.*

W. MACNEILE DIXON

*Just as there are no little people
or unimportant lives, there is
no insignificant work.*

ELENA BONNER

*There are jewels brighter far
Than the sparkling diamonds are;
Jewels never wrought by art,
Nature forms them in the heart.*

JOHN S. ADAMS

*N*othing is ever lost by courtesy. It is the cheapest
of the pleasures; costs nothing and conveys much.
It pleases him who gives and him who receives,
and thus, like mercy, it is twice blessed.

ERASTUS WIMAN

*T*he happiness of life is made up of minute fractions—
the little soon forgotten charities of a kiss or smile,
a kind look, a heartfelt compliment, and the countless
infinitesimals of pleasurable and genial feeling.

SAMUEL TAYLOR COLERIDGE

When First I Called You "Friend"

I don't remember when I first began
To call you "friend.' One day, I only know
The vague companionship that I'd seen grow
So imperceptibly, turned gold, and ran
In tune with all I'd thought or dared to plan.
Since then, you've been to me like music, low,
Yet clear; a fire that throws its warm, bright glow
On me as on each woman, child, and man,
And common thing that lies within its rays;
You've been like wholesome food that stays the cry
Of hungry, groping minds; and like a star—
A self-sufficient star—you make me raise
My utmost being to a higher sky,
In tune, like you, with earth, yet wide, and far.

FLORENCE STEIGERWALT

Kittenhood

Kittenhood, the baby time especially of country cats, is with most the brightest, sprightliest, and prettiest period of their existence, and perhaps the most happy. Bright, meek-eyed, innocent, inquiring little faces, with eager eyes, peep above the basket that is yet their home. One bolder than the others springs out, when, scared at its own audacity, as quickly, and oft clumsily, scrambles back, then out—in—and out, in happy, varied, wild, frolicsome, gambolsome play, they clutch, twist, turn, and wrestle in artless mimicry of desperate quarreling—the struggle over, in liveliest antics they chase and rechase in turn, or in fantastic mood play; 'tis but play, and such wondrous play—bright, joyous, and light; and so life glides on with them as kittens—frisky, skittish, playful kittens.

HARRISON WEIR

Bless This House

Oh Thou, who dwellest in so many homes, possess Thyself of this. Bless the life that is sheltered here. Grant that trust and peace and comfort abide within, and that love and life and usefulness may go out from this home forever.

FAVORITE HOUSE BLESSING OF LADY BIRD JOHNSON